A SOURCE OF STRANGE DELIGHT

A SOURCE OF STRANGE DELIGHT

Poems about the Brontës

Edited by Joy Howard

GREY HEN

Published in 2011 by Grey Hen Press,
PO Box 450
Keighley, W Yorks BD22 9WS

ISBN 978-0-9552952-8-7

Printed by: GB Print & Design,
Loughborough, Leicestershire LE11 1LE

Parsonage

This house is a looking-glass,
the sisters only just
out of the reflection.
The stone floors grained with
sermons and laudanum, the tread
of Byronic heroes and moor-peat.
Their souls laying down layers
of passion in tiny careful script,
the insect-pens scrabbling
from their hive-brain.
This home is a well-worn book,
covers creased with handgrime,
soot, dog-hair, corners
turned down lovingly. That familiar
creak on the stair, turn
of the clock's key, slide
of the sash to shut out
the owl-talk, the choke
of coal smoke, and that call
from the moor.

Char March

The Extra Brontë

I can't imagine writing
at the same table as my sisters,
night after day after night;
that claustrophobia of ink,

words migrating around
the corners of that mahogany.
Osmosis would be a given,
that fire in the eye.

And whose fine story
would I have stolen,
while I waited
for my quill to quicken.

Katrina Naomi

Painted Out

The room where I write is painted green
like an operating theatre, and surgery
sometimes happens here: amputations
of whole stanzas, excisions of words,
the odd tuck that alters the whole picture.

Over my head the Brontë sisters brood,
a postcard of that famous portrait, their faces
barely illuminated by light from one mean
candle in the gloom of a rectory afternoon.
Emily and Charlotte are separated by a pillar

that is their brother, painted out. Their chins
are small, their expressions enigmatic, lips
a uniform pale pink, a hereditary shade,
and eternally pursed. The caption says
by Branwell, but no one seems certain, or why

he painted himself out with a pillar. Under
their serious faces, my own days pass, not quite
as silent as a Yorkshire rectory. Here words
are born and thrive, or age and die ungracefully
while the Brontës look on, give away no secrets.

Wendy Klein

The Brontë Parsonage Museum

Black stones slot one on one
overlap like an insect's carapace
measuring its thorax of chipped scales
up the High Street to this house
armoured still against what once
emerged like birth-wet wings.

Emily's death is held in these walls.
The sofa stages her last breath
over and over for curious eyes. We are distracted
by the irreverence of a red Paisley shawl.
It is as sprightly as fire-flies.

Sue Wood

Ghost Road

Between our house and the parsonage
lorries lumber, tourists trail. You'll find
a hairdresser, chippie, take-away,
newsagent, DIY shop, chemist
and the Haworth Tandoori.

There's an old mill rebuild - ex wool-scouring
city-style apartments; above the tanning studio
a fanlight remembers the Co-op (Registration 88),
long gone. The pub, though, still serves local ale
to working men, and preserves a corner chair
once used by Branwell. This is Brontë country.

Footsteps approach. It's Charlotte and Emily
(Anne left at home, cough bad tonight)
making swift progress up the hill to haul
their wayward brother out the inn,
where he'd been boasting about writing
'Wuthering Heights'. *Eh, th'ahrt a flaysome nowt
reet gaumless* is all he gets.

Homeward their steps weave wavering patterns
back and forth the road, as B leans hard and unpredictable
on either sister's shoulder. They might have liked to stop
for chips or a curry - *now then* - but struggle on
from Mill Hey to Main Street, hustle him indoors
by *t'back-kitchen dooer* where the Reverend Patrick -
with a bit of luck - won't notice.

Wonder what they'd think, now their home's a museum -
their dresses on display - and Ponden Kirk signposted
in Japanese.

Joy Howard

Charlotte Brontë Gets a Laptop

It's grand for those mornings
when you wake to the bullets ricocheting
off the church tower, the groans
of Branwell's going cold turkey,
Emily's infuriating cough.

You draw back the curtains
and by the watery, graveyard light
check you've got the right cigar
for Rochester to smoke in the garden,
the exact number of fatalities
at Cowan Bridge, the legality
of Aunt Reed's last will and testament.

You're responsible for more than half the hits
on friendsreunited
and a quick check of your inbox
confirms your worst fears;
Mme. Heger has put a stop to the emails.

You meant to tinker with chapter 38,
you're not happy with the ending,
but Keeper's howling in the scullery,
Tabitha's banging porridge pans,
Ann reaches for a spittoon
and through the kitchen door
come the unmistakeable tones of that curate.

Carole Bromley

Women Waiting

Each day you came to my class:
butterflies in your silks and chiffons,
you made school colours glow like jewels.
On one trip you explored a Bradford store:
soft materials from India, skeined, folded,
made bright shelves.

The day we went to Haworth
boys filled your conversation:
a few of you already promised,
others had cards, calls, anticipating marriage.

What would Charlotte, in black bombazine,
have made of her young disciples
who stood tall, dark eyes blazing,
vivid veils setting off glossy hair:
my butterflies, scattered across a graveyard,
scarlet, yellow, purple, delicate against the stones.

Below, the dark church reared:
you pressed forward, excited, imagining
Charlotte's wraith, a smiling bride,
waiting in white by the altar side.

For you, white was the colour of mourning.

Thelma Laycock

Swimming with Jane

Thirty wooden chairs revert to orchard.
I watch the bent heads – I've been here before.
Moon-shadows. Night-scents: sweetbriar,
southernwood. Grass slithers under thin shoes.
A huge moth goes humming by. The cigar
draws them on.

It is weeks since they met the girl, hunched
over a book, hiding from the bully:
my flesh shrank when he came near.
Stunted, trembling, intransigent,
she locks them in to her story. I've seen them
thrill at the blow,

trickle of blood – *unjust! unjust!* –
pulsing darkness of the Red Room.
They've lived through the icy dormitory,
burnt porridge, epidemics, grief,
the hoarse laugh in the third storey:
today, though,

is what they've been waiting for, have run back
from swimming to hear, skirts bunched,
hair wisp-tendrilled with damp, shirred
socks: the words they've all seen rising
up the page – *Marry me* – and a voice among the chairs
breathes *oh yes*.

Christine Webb

Here lie the remains of
ANNE BRONTE
DAUGHTER OF THE
REVD P. BRONTE
Incumbent of Haworth Yorkshire
She died Aged 28
MAY 28TH 1849

Scarborough: In Memory of Anne

Sooner or later it seems, each northern poet
pays tribute and tries their Brontë poem.
We thank Heaven for antibiotics,
yet feel the prick of jealousy, tragic death
being a tourist route to fame.
Even the father's grief is commercial,
worth a trip round some church
where once he blessed a child.
Anne we forget. Branwell with his booze
better suits our uneasy time.
Yet on this cliff, with sea and town beneath
it is Anne I think of, the gentle one.

She came here seeking health, and lies in death
apart, as in life. On this wall a plaque
names her grave. That is all.
A late thrush sings; waves whiten sand.
Few come, no one sells souvenirs.
Buried hurriedly and alone
Anne is the legend's footnote.
But she loved her moors too,
hated governessing, burnt with the same fire,
if less intensely. To die so far from home
would be cruel enough; to be eclipsed
by her sisters, a bitter death indeed.

Pauline Kirk

19

'If you had not been with me,
I must have been writing now.'
Charlotte Brontë to her husband, according to Thackeray.

If you were not with me, I would be writing now.
Loneliness would teach me what to say.
I would be sad again. I would remember how

I lived before we met; a house of snow,
wet sky, and shiftless clouds. Red suns by day.
If you were not with me, I would be writing now.

I should leave this room for solitude, so
I might squeeze out rage, weep while my spectres play.
I could be sad again. I could remember how

to spit humiliation through volcano
mouths, spew black torrents at the earth's decay,
if you weren't with me. I should be writing now,

not couched in firelight. I am the friend of owls
and foxes, not small talk and soft ways.
I could be sad again. I still remember how.

You should leave me. You should allow
me silence. Go on, leave. No. Wait. Stay.
If you were not with me, I would be writing now.
I would be sad again. I would remember how.

Marianne Burton

Overnighter

I'm not stupid,
I've danced with the sensors,
know who takes a break
from the tedium of security.

Once the last of the chatter
has broken away, I burrow
behind the Victorian frills
of Reverend Brontë's bed.

I wait for the metal concertina
of shutter to wince its way
to the boards, for the clatter
of court heels on the setts,

for their exhausts to breathe.
I can relax, saunter to the kitchen,
make that kettle angry for tea.
I take my steaming meal through

to the Reverend's dining room,
stab my sausages with his two-
pronged fork, sup my beer
from two dainty glasses. I write

for as long as my candle permits,
take myself to the only decent bed,
put on that stained white nightgown,
place his cap upon my head.

There's no Cathy at the window
and I dream of bad-boy Branwell.

Katrina Naomi

The Smell of Bone

Evening draws in, lies like her grey wool cloak
over the house: its threads limp with damp and cold.
Outside, the sigh of another autumn sounds
at cracked architraves, breathes under rattling door catches.

She has moved closer to the fire.
Her father brings in a squat three-legged stool
before going to his Sunday sermon, unwritten
and Saturday already. He is immersed in redemption.
It burns, flame in his eyes. He places
her stool absently on the hearth-side.
She hears his study door close. Upstairs
Charlotte wraps the counterpane closer
lights a gash of blood-hot fire in her darkest room.
She laughs in silence, her hand stiffening
as the words ignite.

Emily unpins her long hair. The metal presses
too close against skin thinned to worn silk.
Sliding over the thin promontory
that is now her body, her hair glows in the fire-light
tinders firing moorland grass.

Now she picks up the comb her father brought her.
Holding it, she touches her hair with small strokes.
It is so long she tires before reaching her waist.
Holding her hair out in front of her, strand by strand
she calls back the tune of child, girl and woman
from the bright music in its slackening strings.
Her arm shakes. The comb spins.

Emily watches the comb glow red as wayside poppies.
In the fire, the final smell of bone.

Sue Wood

Carole Bromley is a teacher from York. Poems in many magazines. Winner of a number of competitions, including the Bridport. Two pamphlets from Smith/Doorstop: *Unscheduled Halt* 2005 and *Skylight* 2009.

Marianne Burton is working on a PhD on the nineteenth century novel.
Her pamphlet *The Devil's Cut* was a Poetry Book Society Choice. Her first collection is forthcoming from Seren.

Joy Howard lives near Haworth and runs Grey Hen Press. Her poems can be found in anthologies and magazines and online. Collections: *Exit Moonshine* Grey Hen 2009; *Refurbishment* Ward Wood 2011.

Pauline Kirk is the author of two novels, *Waters of Time* and *The Keepers,* and *Foul Play,* and ten poetry collections. A performance poet and editor, she lives in York.

Wendy Klein, U.S-born, has lived most of her life in England. First collection, *Cuba in the Blood* (Cinnamon Press) was published in 2009, and second is due out in 2011.

Thelma Laycock lives in Leeds. Her work has been published in various magazines and anthologies. She has had three pamphlets published and has new collection *A Persistence Of Colour,* (Indigo Dreams Publishing 2011)

Char March is an award-winning poet, playwright and fiction writer. She tutors regularly at Bronte Parsonage. Her credits include four poetry collections, six BBC Radio 4 plays, seven stage plays and numerous short stories

Katrina Naomi is the Brontë Parsonage Museum's first writer-in-residence; a pamphlet, *Charlotte Brontë's Corset*, was published by the Brontë Society in spring 2010.

Christine Webb has published two collections, *After Babel* (Peterloo, 2004) and *Catching Your Breath* (Cinnamon Press, 2011).

Sue Wood has published a pamphlet *Woman Scouring A Pot*(Smith/Doorstop) and a first collection *Imagine Yourself to be Water,* winner of a Cinnamon Press Award for Poetry 2008.